UNIT 10
Against the Odds

INTER·ACTIVE

Mathematics

Activities & Investigations

GLENCOE

McGraw-Hill

New York, New York   Columbus, Ohio   Mission Hills, California   Peoria, Illinois

Send all inquiries to:
Glencoe/McGraw-Hill
936 Eastwind Drive
Westerville, OH 43081

ISBN: 0-02-824512-1 (Student Resource Book)
ISBN: 0-02-824494-X (Teacher's Edition)

3 4 5 6 7 8 9 10 VH/LP 01 00 99 98 97 96

CONTENTS

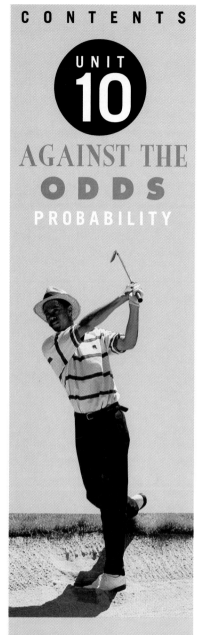

UNIT 10

AGAINST THE ODDS

PROBABILITY

Interdisciplinary Applications

DAVID FOSTER

"The national goal is to develop mathematical power for all students. My vision for learning mathematics includes a student-oriented classroom culture, where students are taking charge of their own learning and are actively engaged in a curriculum that reflects today's world, not the mathematics of 150 years ago."

**Former Teaching Consultant
Middle Grades Mathematics
Renaissance
Morgan Hill, California**
Author of Units 1, 2, 5, 6, 7, 8, 10, 11, 13, 15, 16, 17, and 18

David Foster received his B.A. in mathematics from San Diego State University and has taken graduate courses in computer science at San Jose State University. He has taught mathematics and computer science for nineteen years at the middle school, high school, and college level. Mr. Foster is a founding member of the California Mathematics Project Advisory Committee and was Co-Director of the Santa Clara Valley Mathematics Project. Most recently, he has taken the position of Consulting Author for Glencoe Publishing. Mr. Foster is a member of many professional organizations including the National Council of Teachers of Mathematics and regularly conducts in-service workshops for teachers. He is also the author of a book on computer science.

SANDIE GILLIAM

"Many students only see mathematics as isolated number facts and formulas to memorize. By using this program, which incorporates the mathematics into a context of large, real-life units tied together with literature, science, and history, the middle school student can find meaning in the mathematics."

**Mathematics Teacher
San Lorenzo Valley High School
Felton, California**
Co-author of Unit 14

Sandie Gilliam received her B.A. from San Jose State University and is a mentor teacher and instructor for the Monterey Bay Area Mathematics Project. She was a semi-finalist for the Presidential Award for Excellence in the Teaching of Mathematics in the state of California. Ms. Gilliam has served as a consultant for the California Department of Education and many local school districts and county offices of education. She is a member of the National Council of Teachers of Mathematics and is a frequent speaker at conferences and teacher in-service workshops. Ms. Gilliam was a writer and consultant for Glencoe's *Investigating Mathematics: An Interactive Approach.*

JACK PRICE

"This program is designed to help students become mathematically powerful as they develop problem-solving skills and self-reliance, as well as the ability to work well with others. At the same time, they will strengthen their basic skills and be exposed to new and exciting ideas in mathematics."

**Co-Director, Center for Science
and Mathematics Education
California State Polytechnic
University
Pomona, California**
Author of Unit 3

Jack Price received his B.A. from Eastern Michigan University and his Doctorate in Mathematics Education from Wayne State University. Dr. Price has been active in mathematics education for over 40 years, 38 of those years at grades K through 12. In his current position, he teaches mathematics and methods courses for preservice teachers and consults with school districts on curriculum change. He is president of the National Council of Teachers of Mathematics, is a frequent speaker at professional conferences, conducts many teacher in-service workshops, and is an author of numerous mathematics instructional materials.

INTERACTIVE MATHEMATICS AUTHORS

KAY McCLAIN

"Building conceptual understanding in mathematics challenges us to re-define what it means to know and do mathematics. This program was developed to allow teachers to become facilitators of learning while students explore and investigate mathematics — strengthening their understanding and stimulating interest."

Kay McClain

Doctoral Candidate
George Peabody College
Vanderbilt University
Nashville, Tennessee
Author of Unit 9, Co-author of Unit 14

Kay McClain received her B.A. from Auburn University and her Educational Specialist degree from the University of Montevallo in Montevallo, Alabama. While a teacher at Mountain Brook Middle School in Birmingham, she received the Presidential Award for Excellence in the Teaching of Mathematics in the state of Alabama. Ms. McClain is a Woodrow Wilson fellow and a member of the National Council of Teachers of Mathematics. She regularly conducts teacher in-service workshops and is a frequent speaker at local, state, and national mathematics education conferences. She is also an author of middle school mathematics instructional materials.

BARNEY MARTINEZ

"Students learn mathematics best when their teacher enables them to become actively involved in worthwhile mathematical investigations. Students should be encouraged to interact with each other. Then, through their collaborative efforts, students build their own understanding of mathematics."

Barney Martinez

Mathematics Teacher
Jefferson High School
Daly City, California
Co-Author of Unit 12

Barney Martinez received his B.S. in mathematics from The University of San Francisco and is an instructor of pre-service mathematics teachers at the College of Notre Dame in Belmont, California. Mr. Martinez currently serves on the Mathematics Development Team of the California Department of Education and the Pursuing Excellence Revision Advisory Committee. He is a member of the National Council of Teachers of Mathematics and is very active as a speaker and workshop leader at professional development conferences.

LINDA DRITSAS

"This program is designed to encourage students to be creative and inventive, while gaining mathematical power. Open-ended situations and investigations provide the setting that allows students to work at varying depths, while nurturing their natural curiosity to learn."

Linda Dritsas

Mathematics Coordinator
Fresno Unified School District
Fresno, California
Author of Unit 4, Co-author of Unit 12

Linda Dritsas received her B.A. and M.A. from California State University at Fresno. She taught middle school mathematics for many years and, for two years, taught mathematics at California State University at Fresno. Ms. Dritsas has been the Central Section President of the California Mathematics Council and is a member of the National Council of Teachers of Mathematics and the Association for Supervision and Curriculum Development. She frequently conducts mathematics teacher in-service workshops and is an author of numerous mathematics instructional materials, including those for middle school students and teachers.

CONTRIBUTORS INTERACTIVE MATHEMATICS

Each of the Consultants read all 18 units while each Reviewer read one unit. The Consultants and Reviewers gave suggestions for improving the Student Resource Books, Teacher's Editions, Cooperative Group Cards, Posters, and Transparencies. The Writers wrote the Student Diversity Strategies that appear in the Teacher's Edition.

CONSULTANTS

Dr. Judith Jacobs, *Units 1-18*
  Director, Center for Science
    and Mathematics Education
  California State
    Polytechnic University
  Pomona, California

Dr. Cleo M. Meek, *Units 1-18*
  Mathematics Consultant,
  Retired
  North Carolina Dept. of
    Public Instruction
  Raleigh, North Carolina

Beatrice Moore-Harris,
  Units 1-18
  College Board Equity 2000
    Site Coordinator
  Fort Worth Independent
    School District
  Fort Worth, Texas

Deborah J. Murphy, *Units 1-18*
  Mathematics Teacher
  Killingsworth Jr. High School,
  ABC Unified School District
  Cerritos, California

Javier Solorzano, *Units 1-18*
  Mathematics Teacher
  South El Monte High School
  South El Monte, California

WRITERS

Student Diversity
Teacher's Edition

Dr. Gilbert J. Cuevas
  Professor of Mathematics
    Education
  University of Miami
  Coral Gables, Florida

Sally C. Mayberry, *Ed.D.*
  Assistant Professor
    Mathematics/Science
    Education
  St. Thomas University
  Miami, Florida

REVIEWERS

John W. Anson, *Unit 11*
  Mathematics Teacher
  Arroyo Seco Junior High
    School
  Valencia, California

Laura Beckwith, *Unit 13*
  Mathematics Department
    Chairperson
  William James Middle School
  Fort Worth, Texas

Betsy C. Blume, *Unit 6*
  Vice Principal/
    Director of Curriculum
  Valleyview Middle School
  Denville, New Jersey

James F. Bohan, *Unit 11*
  Mathematics K-12 Program
    Coordinator
  Manheim Township School
    District
  Lancaster, Pennsylvania

Dr. Carol Fry Bohlin, *Unit 14*
  Director, San Joaquin Valley
    Mathematics Project
  Associate Professor,
    Mathematics Education
  California State University,
    Fresno
  Fresno, California

David S. Bradley, *Unit 9*
  Mathematics
    Teacher/Department
    Chairperson
  Jefferson Jr. High
  Kearns, Utah

Dr. Diane Briars, *Unit 9*
  Mathematics Specialist
  Pittsburgh City Schools
  Pittsburgh, Pennsylvania

Jackie Britton, *Unit 18*
Mathematics Teacher
V. W. Miller Intermediate
Pasadena, Texas

Sybil Y. Brown, *Unit 8*
Mathematics Teacher
Franklin Alternative Middle
School
Columbus, Ohio

Blanche Smith Brownley, *Unit 18*
Supervising Director of
Mathematics (Acting)
District of Columbia Public
Schools
Washington, D.C.

Bruce A. Camblin, *Unit 7*
Mathematics Teacher
Weld School District 6
Greeley, Colorado

Cleo Campbell, *Unit 15*
Coordinator of Mathematics,
K-12
Anne Arundel County
Public Schools
Annapolis, Maryland

Savas Carabases, *Unit 13*
Mathematics Supervisor
Camden City School District
Camden City, New Jersey

W. Karla Castello, *Unit 6*
Mathematics Teacher
Yerba Buena High School
San Jose, California

Diane M. Chase, *Unit 16*
Mathematics Teacher/
Department Chairperson
Pacific Jr. High School
Vancouver, Washington

Dr. Phyllis Zweig Chinn, *Unit 9*
Professor of Mathematics
Humboldt State University
Arcata, California

Nancy W. Crowther, *Unit 17*
Mathematics Teacher
Sandy Springs Middle School
Atlanta, Georgia

Regina F. Cullen, *Unit 13*
Supervisor of Mathematics
West Essex Regional Schools
North Caldwell, New Jersey

Sara J. Danielson, *Unit 17*
Mathematics Teacher
Albany Middle School
Albany, California

Lorna Denman, *Unit 10*
Mathematics Teacher
Sunny Brae Middle School
Arcata, California

Richard F. Dube, *Unit 4*
Mathematics Supervisor
Taunton High School
Taunton, Massachusetts

Mary J. Dubsky, *Unit 1*
Mathematics Curriculum
Specialist
Baltimore City Public Schools
Baltimore, Maryland

Dr. Leo Edwards, *Unit 5*
Director, Mathematics/
Science Education Center
Fayetteville State University
Fayetteville, North Carolina

Connie Fairbanks, *Unit 7*
Mathematics Teacher
South Whittier Intermediate
School
Whittier, California

Ana Marina C. Gomezgil, *Unit 15*
District Translator/Interpreter
Sweetwater Union
High School District
Chula Vista, California

Sandy R. Guerra, *Unit 9*
Mathematics Teacher
Harry H. Rogers Middle
School
San Antonio, Texas

Rick Hall, *Unit 4*
Curriculum Coordinator
San Bernardino County
Superintendent of Schools
San Bernardino, California

Carolyn Hansen, *Unit 14*
Instructional Specialist
Williamsville Central Schools
Williamsville, New York

Jenny Hembree, *Unit 8*
Mathematics Teacher
Shelby Co. East Middle
School
Shelbyville, Kentucky

Susan Hertz, *Unit 16*
Mathematics Teacher
Paul Revere Middle School
Houston, Texas

Janet L. Hollister, *Unit 5*
Mathematics Teacher
LaCumbre Middle School
Santa Barbara, California

Dorothy Nachtigall Hren, *Unit 12*
Mathematics Teacher/
Department Chairperson
Northside Middle School
Norfolk, Virginia

Grace Hutchings, *Unit 3*
Mathematics Teacher
Parkman Middle School
Woodland Hills, California

Lyle D. Jensen, *Unit 18*
Mathematics Teacher
Albright Middle School
Villa Park, Illinois

CONTRIBUTORS INTERACTIVE MATHEMATICS

Robert R. Jones, *Unit 7*
Chief Consultant,
Mathematics, Retired
North Carolina Department
of Public Instruction
Raleigh, North Carolina

Mary Kay Karl, *Unit 3*
Mathematics Coordinator
Community Consolidated
School District 54
Schaumburg, Illinois

Janet King, *Unit 14*
Mathematics Teacher
North Gulfport Junior High
Gulfport, Mississippi

Franca Koeller, *Unit 17*
Mathematics Mentor Teacher
Arroyo Seco Junior High
School
Valencia, California

Louis La Mastro, *Unit 2*
Mathematics/Computer
Science Teacher
North Bergen High School
North Bergen, New Jersey

Patrick Lamberti, *Unit 6*
Supervisor of Mathematics
Toms River Schools
Toms River, New Jersey

Dr. Betty Larkin, *Unit 14*
Mathematics Coordinator
K - 12
Lee County School District
Fort Myers, Florida

Ann Lawrence, *Unit 1*
Mathematics
Teacher/Department
Coordinator
Mountain Brook Jr. High
School
Mountain Brook, Alabama

Catherine Louise Marascalco,
Unit 3
Mathematics Teacher
Southaven Elementary
School
Southaven, Mississippi

Dr. Hannah Masterson, *Unit 10*
Mathematics Specialist
Suffolk Board of
Cooperative Education
Dix Hills, New York

Betty Monroe Nelson, *Unit 8*
Mathematics Teacher
Blackburn Middle School
Jackson, Mississippi

Dale R. Oliver, *Unit 2*
Assistant Professor of
Mathematics
Humboldt State University
Arcata, California

Carol A. Pudlin, *Unit 4*
Mathematics Teacher/
Consultant
Griffiths Middle School
Downey, California

Diane Duggento Sawyer,
Unit 15
Mathematics Chairperson
Exeter Area Junior High
Exeter, New Hampshire

Donald W. Scheuer, Jr., *Unit 12*
Mathematics Department
Chairperson
Abington Junior High
Abington, Pennsylvania

Linda S. Shippey, *Unit 8*
Mathematics Teacher
Bondy Intermediate School
Pasadena, Texas

Barbara Smith, *Unit 1*
Mathematics Supervisor,
K-12
Unionville-Chadds Ford
School District
Kennett Square, Pennsylvania

Stephanie Z. Smith, *Unit 14*
Project Assistant
University of Wisconsin-
Madison
Madison, Wisconsin

Dora M. Swart, *Unit 11*
Mathematics Teacher
W. F. West High School
Chehalis, Washington

Ciro J. Tacinelli, Sr., *Unit 8*
Curriculum Director:
Mathematics
Hamden Public Schools
Hamden, Connecticut

Kathy L. Terwelp, *Unit 12*
K-8 Mathematics Supervisor
Summit Public Schools
Summit, New Jersey

Marty Terzieff, *Unit 18*
Secondary Math Curriculum
Chairperson
Mead Junior High School
Mead, Washington

Linda L. Walker, *Unit 18*
Mathematics Teacher
Cobb Middle School
Tallahassee, Florida

AGAINST THE ODDS

Looking Ahead

In this unit, you will see how mathematics can be used in determining fairness and probability. You will experience:

▶ solving problems involving probability and fairness

▶ determining probability ratios and probability values

▶ designing random-generating spinners

▶ designing games to meet certain specifications

▶ exploring odds, probability, and actual outcome

Did You Ever Wonder?

What do mathematics and the game of golf have to do with each other? Turn the page and see how Tiger Woods of Cypress, California, combines the two.

Teens in the News

Featuring: Tiger Woods
Age: 17
Hometown: Cypress, California
Career Goal: Professional Golfer
Interests: Conducting Golf Clinics

If there is such a thing as a born golfer, Tiger Woods is one. He has been "playing" golf since he was 9 months old! At 11 months, he began hitting golf balls into a net with a toy club. Now, at age 17, Tiger hopes to become a professional golfer!

Tiger has been taking lessons from golf pros since he was 4 years old. He has traveled to Michigan, New York, Ohio, Pennsylvania, and Texas to play in amateur tournaments. *Golf Week Magazine* and *Golf Digest* have named Tiger amateur player of the year. He was the number-one-ranked Junior Player in the United States two years in a row!

Tiger says mathematics is a big part of the game of golf. Golf clubs vary by length, weight, shape, and size. He must consider variables like distance to the hole, wind speed, elevation of the hole, and the lie of the ball to know which club to use. Tiger does this type of calculation many times during a game because the conditions on the golf course change with each shot.

Tiger's expertise has already paid off. He will attend college on a golf scholarship. Tiger wants to earn a degree in accounting. He has seen too many professionals lose their money as a result of poor business management.

Tiger wants to wisely manage the money that he earns as a professional golfer.

Golf's gender gap

The top female golfer now earns about $\frac{3}{4}$ as much as her male counterpart.

$1,165,477
Top PGA earnings

$863,578
Top LPGA earnings

$75,262

$16,892   '60   '70   '80   '90

Source: LPGA, PGA

Team Project

Your Best Shot

The best shot Tiger or any golfer can have is a hole-in-one. Research to discover the odds of getting a hole-in-one. Based on those odds, how many rounds of golf would you have to play to get one? Do you think the odds of a hole-in-one at miniature golf are better or worse than the odds of a hole-in-one at regular golf? Explain your answer.

1744

Oldest organized golf club founded in Leith, England.

1900

Golf became an Olympic sport.

Tiger Woods ranked Number One Junior Golfer

1992

1800

1900

2000

1700

Mary, Queen of Scots, coined the name "caddie".

1860

Alan Shepard played golf on the moon.

1971

For more information

If you would like more information about the game of golf, contact:

**UNITED STATES GOLF ASSOCIATION
BOX 708
Far Hills, New Jersey 07931**

You can learn more about the math Tiger may use to determine his odds of winning a golf tournament by completing the activities in this unit.

Setting the Scene

MATHEMATICS TOOLKIT

Many professions require the use of tools. This mathematics toolkit includes tools you may find useful in this unit. At times you may feel lost and/or not know where to begin when presented with a problem situation. Take time to read this toolkit to see how the characters in the script used probability to solve their problem. You don't need to wait until your teacher tells you to make a chart or create a list. Instead, if it seems like it might help, try it.

Narrator: Emilio, Tom, and Yuji are friends. They are middle schoolers who love to play basketball.

Emilio: Hey, did you see the contest at the Shoelocker in the mall?

Tom: Yeah, it's all over the radio.

Emilio: You can win the Airborne-Rikees. They're $120 shoes!

Yuji: Yeah, those are great basketball shoes. They're worn by all the best basketball players.

Emilio: I know. And I'm going to win that contest!

Yuji: How are you going to pull that off?

Tom: Yeah, you know it's pure luck whoever wins.

Emilio: I've got a plan. You'll see.

Yuji: You've got to be kidding. You don't have a chance.

Emilio: Okay, but when I wear those Airborne-Rikees to our next game, don't be surprised!

Yuji: So, what's the big secret? Let's hear this plan.

Emilio: No way! You'll try to copy and blow my chances.

Yuji: We won't copy. Right, Tom?

Tom: Yeah, we promise. It probably won't work anyway...unless you cheat.

Emilio: I'm not going to cheat. I figured out how to do it mathematically.

Tom: So, tell us.

Emilio: Well, in Ms. Washington's math class, we're studying probability. We learned last week that if you have more entries in a contest than anyone else, then you have the best chance of winning.

Tom: So how are you going to get more entries than anyone else?

Emilio: Easy. The contest rules state that you can enter as many times as you like.

Yuji: Yeah, but it will cost you $2.00 per entry.

Emilio: Well, I've saved up $50 to buy those shoes. If I use that money in the contest, I can buy 25 tickets for that amount. That means my chances of winning are 25 times as great as the person who buys just one ticket. So I can get those Airborne-Rikees for just $50 and save $70 plus tax!

Tom: I don't know. Something doesn't sound right about that.

Emilio: Well, just ask your math teacher whether I have a good plan. But remember it's *my* plan. No copying...you promised!

Stop the Script!
Determine whether Emilio has a good plan. How could you determine his chances of winning? Would it be worth it?

Narrator: The students meet during lunch the next day. They start talking about the contest again.

Tom: So, Emilio, have you paid for your 25 contest entries yet?

Emilio: I'm going down to the mall after school today to ensure my victory.

Yuji: I think you should think about it more. I talked to my mom, and she said that it could backfire on you.

Emilio: Why is that? I bet you just don't want me to win. You're jealous that I thought of this plan first.

Yuji: No, it's not that. My mom said you don't know how many people are entering the contest and having 25 entries may not make a lot of difference if there are a lot of entries. Plus, someone could luck out and win with just one ticket.

Emilio: Yeah, but I still think having 25 tickets will give me a pretty good chance of winning.

Tom: Well, before you go and spend your money, my brother's friend works at the Shoelocker, and maybe I can find out how many entries there are. Why don't you wait until tomorrow?

Emilio: All right. But the contest closes tomorrow, so I can only wait one day.

Narrator: Tom talked with his brother's friend who works at the Shoelocker.

Emilio: What did your brother's friend tell you?

Tom: Well, he didn't know exactly, but he heard the store manager say that they have earned about $3,000 in the contest. That must mean they have about 1,500 entries.

Emilio: That's lots of entries...but is that good news or bad news?

Yuji: I know how to figure that out. We can find the probability of you winning by dividing the number of times you entered by the total number of entries.

If you buy 25 tickets, you will have 25 chances of winning. If there are 1,500 entries and you buy 25 tickets, there will be a total of 1,525 entries.

The probability of you winning, then, is $\frac{25}{1,525}$. If we divide that on a calculator, we get 0.01639.

Emilio: What does that mean? Is 0.01639 good or bad?

Tom: Well, it's not real good. The best probability is 1, or 100%. That would happen if you were the only one who entered the contest. The probability of you winning would be $\frac{25}{25}$, or 1.

The worst probability is 0. That would happen if you didn't enter at all. The probability of you winning would be $\frac{0}{1,500}$, or 0.

Emilio: So, you're saying probability is a number between 0 and 1.

Tom: Yes.

Yuji: And a 50-50 chance of winning would be a probability of 0.50.

Emilio: Hmmm. My probability is less than 0.02. That looks real bad. I don't want to throw my money away. Maybe I should go ask Ms. Washington what to do.

Narrator: Emilio goes to see his math teacher, Ms. Washington, and explains the situation to her.

Ms. Washington: Well, Emilio, I don't want to tell you how to spend your money, but I will show you how people use mathematics to help them make decisions regarding chance.

Emilio: Okay, maybe that will help me make up my mind.

Ms. Washington: What I'm going to show you is called **expected value**. Expected value helps us to determine what is most likely to happen.

You and your friends have already done most of the work. You have calculated that your probability is 0.01639. That means you will win a little less than 2% of the time.

Emilio: Let's just round off and use 2% then.

Ms. Washington: Okay. So tell me, what's your chance of losing?

Emilio: The total of either winning or losing is 100%. So, 100% − 2% = 98%. My chances of losing are 98%. Boy, that's pretty bad.

Ms. Washington: Yes. But remember, there's still the possibility that you could win $120 shoes for just $50.

Emilio: So how do price and cost work into this problem?

Ms. Washington: Well, that's where expected value comes in. First, you need to determine your expected value of *winning*. That is 2% times the amount you win, $120. That equals $2.40.

Next, you need to determine the expected value of *losing*. That is 98% times the $50 you would pay. That equals $49.

When you compare these two amounts, you find that on the average you will lose $49.00 − $2.40, or $46.60, every time you enter a contest using your plan of buying 25 tickets.

Emilio: Boy, I almost threw away my hard-earned money!

Ms. Washington: It's true that a person can be lucky, and of course, someone *will* win the contest, but you need to be careful about how much you risk because the odds are against you.

Emilio: I'm going to tell my friends that they saved me from losing all my money. But, I think I might go to the mall and enter once. You never know, I might be lucky!

This concludes the Mathematics Toolkit. It included many mathematical tools for you to use throughout this unit. As you work through this unit, you should use these tools to help you solve problems. You may want to explain how to use these mathematical tools in your journal. Or you may want to create a toolkit notebook to add mathematical tools you discover throughout this unit.

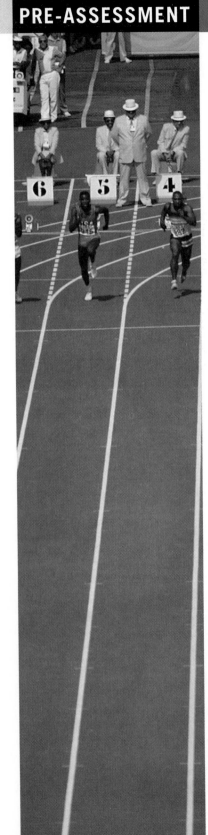

WHAT'S FAIR ABOUT THIS?

You work for a game manufacturer and it's your job to determine whether a certain new board game is fair or unfair. The game involves a track meet in which four racers (four players) are trying to make it to the finish line first.

Racer	Numbers
Racer A	3 or 4
Racer B	5 or 6
Racer C	7 or 8
Racer D	9 or 10
All racers move two spaces on 2, 11, or 12.	

To play, roll a pair of number cubes and add the numbers on the number cubes. The sum of the number cubes will match one of the racer's numbers in the table above. That racer moves three spaces and all the other racers move only one space. If the sum of the number cubes is 2, 11, or 12, then all players move two spaces. Take turns rolling the number cubes until one player reaches the finish line. The racer to reach the finish line first wins the race.

Play the game several times and record which racer wins each time. Determine whether the game is fair or unfair. Use the poster board or blank transparency provided by your teacher to write a report of your findings.

Game Fair
Quick on the Draw

This game is for two players. Select who will be Player A and Player B.

Each player places his or her tile at the starting line. Shuffle the deck of cards. One player draws a card. If a face card is drawn, Player A moves his or her tile two spaces on the game board. If an ace or a number card is drawn, Player B moves his or her tile one space on the game board.

Players alternate drawing a card until one player's tile reaches the finish line. That player wins the game.

MENU station B

Number Cubes

This game is for two players. Select who will be Player A and Player B.

Each player places his or her tile at the starting line. One player rolls the number cubes. If the sum of the number cubes is an even number, Player A moves his or her tile one space on the game board. If the sum of the number cubes is an odd number, Player B moves his or her tile one space on the game board.

Players alternate rolling the number cubes until one player's tile reaches the finish line. That player wins the game.

Coin Toss

MENU
station
C

This game is for three players. Select who will be Player A, Player B, and Player C.

Each player places his or her tile at the starting line. One player tosses the coins. If the coins are both heads, Player A moves his or her tile one space on the game board. If the coins are a head and a tail, Player B moves his or her tile one space. If the coins are both tails, then player C moves his or her tile one space.

Players alternate tossing the coins until one player's tile reaches the finish line. That player wins the game.

MENU station
D

FLIP THE CHIPS

This game is for two players. Select who will be Player A and Player B.

Each player places his or her tile at the starting line. One player flips the chips. If the chips are both red, Player A moves his or her tile one space on the game board. If the chips are red and yellow, Player B moves his or her tile one space on the game board.

Players alternate flipping the chips until one player's tile reaches the finish line. That player wins the game.

Don't Lose Your Marbles

M E N U
s t a t i o n

This game is for three players. Select who will be Player A, Player B, and Player C.

Each player places his or her tile at the starting line. One player picks a marble from the bag. If the marble is red, Player A moves his or her tile one space on the game board. If the marble is yellow, Player B moves his or her tile one space. If the marble is blue, then Player C moves his or her tile one space. The marble is returned to the bag.

Players alternate picking a marble and returning it to the bag until one player's tile reaches the finish line. That player wins the game.

Probable Cause
What if....

- You took a survey of 50 adults and found that 15 of them smoke. If you were to randomly select one of the 50 people to interview, what is the probability that the person you select is a *nonsmoker*? Explain how you determined your answer.

- You put three blue marbles, four red marbles, and seven yellow marbles into a bag and shake the bag. You ask your friend to select a marble from the bag without looking. What is the probability that your friend selects a yellow marble? Explain how you determined your answer.

- You have a standard deck of playing cards. After shuffling the deck of cards, you pick one card. What is the probability that the card you pick is *not* an ace or a face card? Explain how you determined your answer.

- You roll three number cubes. What is the probability that the sum of the numbers on the number cubes is 15, 16, 17, or 18? Explain how you determined your answer.

- You have two chips. One chip is red on both sides, the other chip is red on one side and yellow on the other side. You put the chips in a cup, shake the cup, and spill the chips onto the table. What is the probability that at least one chip will show red? Explain how you determined your answer.

It Happened by Chance

Pick a card from the deck of fraction cards provided by your teacher. The fraction on the card represents a probability.

Think about situations in which events happen by chance. Write a paragraph describing a situation that involves the probability on the card you picked. Include any illustrations you may need to describe your situation. You can write your paragraph as a story if you would like.

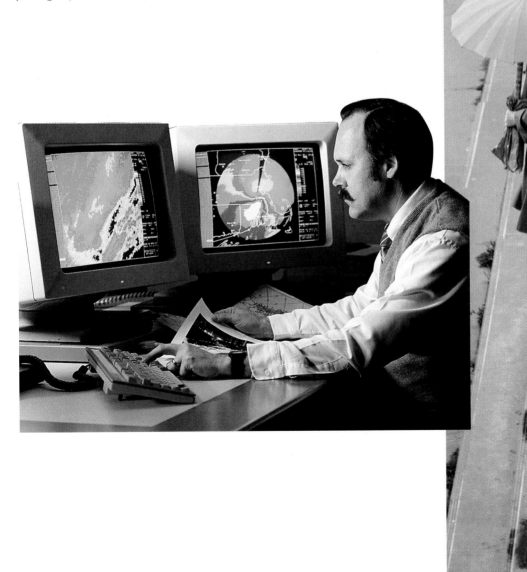

THE BIG SPIN
Round and Round it Goes....

Your teacher will provide your group with a set of clue cards. Each member of your group should select one clue card and hold onto it throughout the activity. You may not hand your card to anyone else. However, you may read it to your group members as many times as necessary.

As a group, use the clues on the cards to design a random-generating spinner. Once you have designed your spinner, use the clue cards to verify that you built a spinner that satisfies all the clues.

When your group has completed designing the spinner and verified its accuracy, each student should draw a model of the spinner to scale using a compass, protractor, pencil, and paper. Refer to the group card entitled *How to Build a Spinner* if you need help. Label each section of the spinner with the number of that section and its probability. Describe in writing the process your group used in designing the spinner and how you know it is accurate.

When your group has completed the first spinner, exchange clue cards with another group and repeat these instructions for a new spinner. You will continue to design spinners and exchange clue cards until you have five different spinners.

HOW TO BUILD A SPINNER

Cut a blank piece of paper into a square. Using a compass, draw a circle in the square. Mark the center of the circle with a dot.

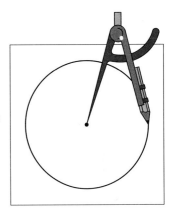

To make a spinner you need to divide the circle into fractional parts called **sectors**. A sector of a circle is shaped like a piece of pie. Since there are 360 degrees (360°) in a circle, multiply each fraction by 360 to find the number of degrees in each sector of the spinner.

Example

Suppose you want a sector of a spinner to be $\frac{1}{3}$ of a circle.

To find out how many degrees this would be, multiply 360° by $\frac{1}{3}$. The central angle of the sector is 120°.

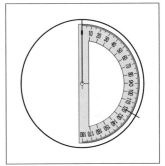

To draw a sector of 120°, draw a vertical line from the center of the circle to a point on the circle. This is a **radius** of the circle. Place a protractor on this radius with its center at the center of the circle. There are two scales on the protractor. Use the one that begins with 0° where the radius aligns with the protractor. Follow the scale from the 0° point to the 120° point. Make a small mark at this point and draw a line from the center of the circle through this point to a point on the circle. This is another radius of the circle.

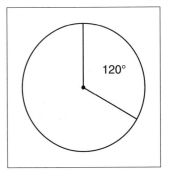

One way to make this sectored circle into a spinner is to place a pencil with a paper clip or bobby pin on its tip at the center of the circle and to spin the paper clip or bobby pin using your free hand.

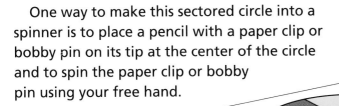

Play to Win

You are a game designer. Your boss has challenged you to design a game where one player has a definite advantage over the other player(s). She feels the company can market the game to people who are poor sports and always want to win.

The game needs to be designed in such a way that it is not obvious to the other player(s) that one player has an advantage. Your game may be a board game, a card game, or any other type of game. You can use any random-generating device you want. Your game may be designed so that the same player wins most of the time or all of the time. The game with the best design is the game in which the other players don't catch on too early that it is unfair.

Once you have come up with your design, write down the rules to the game. Include a special section on how the winning player has the advantage. Explain in those remarks the probability of that player winning the game and how you determined that value.

Share your game with others in the class. After playing the game a few times, have your challengers try to determine your winning strategy and the probability of you winning. Then switch roles, having one of your challengers become the player with the advantage. In these roles, do you get the same outcome?

After examining one designer's game, switch games and test a new game following the same procedure.

Odds and Ends
Spinning Out of Control

This game is for three players. Use the spinner and score cards provided by your teacher. Each player chooses a color: red, blue or green.

One player spins the spinner. If the spinner comes up red, then the red player places a tally mark in the win (W) column, and the blue and green players each place a tally mark in the loss (L) column. If the spinner comes up blue or green, the player whose color comes up tallies a win, and the other two tally a loss.

Spin the spinner 50 times. Write a ratio comparing your wins to your losses. This is your odds of winning the game. Using all three players' results, determine the probability of getting red, green, or blue on a single spin.

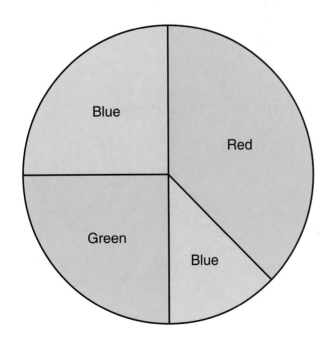

Some Sums

This game is for three players. Use the two number cubes, three different-colored tiles, and game board provided by your teacher. Players move their tile on the game board according to the following rules.

- Player A moves one space when a sum of 1, 2, 3, or 4 occurs.
- Player B moves one space when a sum of 5, 6, 7, or 8 occurs.
- Player C moves one space when a sum of 9, 10, 11, or 12 occurs.

Begin with three tiles at the starting line of the game board. Have one player roll the number cubes. Find the sum of the numbers on the two number cubes and move the appropriate tile one space on the game board. The first player to have his or her tile reach the finish line wins.

Play the game 12 times. Each player should keep track of the number of games won and the number of games lost.

Determine the odds of each player winning. Then determine the probability of each player winning. Describe in writing how the odds are related to the probability.

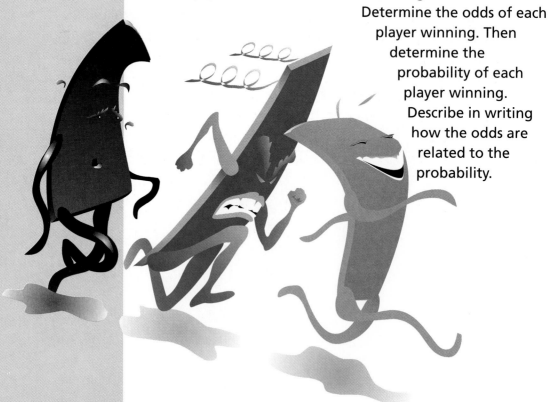

HOW THE CHIPS FALL

This game is for three players. Use the three two-colored chips, cup, three different-colored tiles, and game board provided by your teacher. Players move their tiles according to the following rules.

- Player A moves one space when the chips show exactly two red sides.

- Player B moves one space when the chips show *at least* two yellow sides.

- Player C moves one space when the chips are all the same color.

Begin with three tiles at the starting line. One player shakes the chips in the cup and pours them out. Based on how the chips fall, move the tile of Player A, B, or C one space on the game board. Notice that there are cases when two tiles may move on the same turn. The first player to have his or her tile reach the finish line wins.

Play 16 games. Each player should keep track of the number of games won and the number of games lost. Determine the odds of each player winning. Find the theoretical odds and compare to your experimental odds. Describe this comparison in writing.

Stack the Deck

This game is for three players. Use the deck of cards, game board, and three different-colored tiles provided by your teacher. Players move their tiles according to the following rules.

- Player A moves one space when a face card is drawn.
- Player B moves one space when a red card is drawn.
- Player C moves one space when an even number (not a face card) is drawn.

One player draws a card. Depending on what card is drawn, Player A, B, or C moves his or her tile one space on the game board. Notice that there are cases when two tiles may move on the same turn. The first player to have his or her tile reach the finish line wins.

Play 20 games. Each player should keep track of the number of games won and the number of games lost. Determine the odds of each player winning. Find the theoretical odds and compare to your experimental odds. Describe this comparison in writing.

Name That Game

Design a spinner that produces a game situation having the following odds.

- Player A: 1 to 2
- Player B: 1 to 5
- Player C: 5 to 7
- Player D: 1 to 11

Play the game several times. Compare your actual outcomes to the odds stated above. Determine the probability of each player winning the game. Write about your findings.

SPINNER WINNER

An Odd Situation

Describe a situation outside of school that involves using odds. You may need to research a topic using newspapers or magazines. Write about the situation, list the odds given for that situation, and determine the probability of the situation occurring.

EVENING THE ODDS

Game 1

This game is for three players. It is played with two coins and a cup. The object of the game is for a player to get 25 points.

The number of points a player receives for a win is called a payoff value. The payoff values are as follows.

- Player A gets 2 points each time two heads occur.
- Player B gets 2 points each time two tails occur.
- Player C gets 1 point each time a head and a tail occur.

Players alternate shaking the coins in the cup and spilling them out on the table. Play this game several times and record your results. Is it a fair game for all the players? Justify your answer.

Game 2

This game is for two players. It is played with a deck of cards. The object of the game is for a player to get 50 points.

The payoff values are as follows.

- Player A gets 4 points each time an ace or face card is picked.
- Player B gets 2 points each time a numbered card is picked.

Shuffle the deck of cards and cut the deck. Players alternate picking the top card of the deck. Play this game several times and record your results. Is it a fair game for both players? Justify your answer.

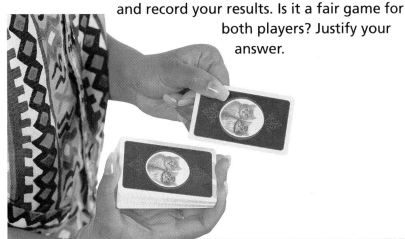

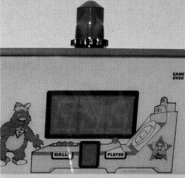

Game 3

This game is for three players. It is played with two number cubes. The object of the game is for a player to get 50 points.
    The payoff values are as follows.

* Player A gets 5 points each time the sum of the number cubes is 7.
* Player B gets 2 points each time the sum of the number cubes is greater than 7.
* Player C gets 2 points each time the sum of the number cubes is less than 7.

    Alternate rolling the number cubes. Play this game several times and record your results. Is it a fair game for all the players? Justify your answer.

Game 4

This game is for any number of players. It is played with a spinner. Using paper, a compass, and a protractor, make a spinner like the one shown below.
    The object of this game is for a player to get 50 points. Points are awarded to the player according to his or her spin. Players alternate spinning the spinner and determining their points.
    Play this game several times. Is it a fair game for all the players? Justify your answer.

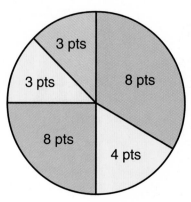

Game Time

Design your own game. Select a random-generating device and a game objective. Determine a payoff value for the occurrence of each possible event.

Determine whether or not your game is fair. If your game is fair, justify your conclusion. If your game gives certain players an advantage, determine how much of an advantage or disadvantage each player has.

Write about your game. Describe the process you used to determine whether the game is fair and who may have an advantage. Discuss why you believe you have accurately predicted whether the game is fair or not.

Share your game with a classmate or classmates (depending on how many are needed to play your game). Explain the rules to your classmate(s), and let them choose which players they prefer to be. Play your game several times to test your conclusions. Are your conclusions correct? Justify your answer.

COMPUTER investigation

Chances Are

The computer program "Chances" allows you to "play" several rounds of a game in a short amount of time. Each round is called an **event**.

The computer asks you to input the number of players involved in each game. It then assigns a probability of winning and a payoff value to each player. Your task is to run three or four games and to determine if the games are fair or unfair for each player. The following instructions allow you to use the computer program "Chances."

1. Boot up the BASIC program.
2. Load the "Chances" program by typing: LOAD "CHANCES"
3. Run the program by typing: RUN
4. The program will ask the question:
   HOW MANY PLAYERS (2 TO 9)?
   Enter the number of players you wish to use in the game.

The program plays 25 events at a time. It reports back a summary of how many points each player gets for a win (the payoff value), how many wins each player has, how many points each player has, and the percent of the total points each player has.

Have the computer play as many events as you need to in order to determine whether the game is fair or unfair for each player.

Once you have arrived at your conclusions for the first game, try a different game. Determine whether this game is fair or unfair for each player. Repeat this process for at least one more game.

Record the results of all the games you played. Write a report summarizing your findings. Explain how you arrived at your conclusions and what process you used. Give specific examples to support your findings. Illustrate your findings with graphs, diagrams, or other pictorial representations of the data. Be prepared to discuss your report with the class.

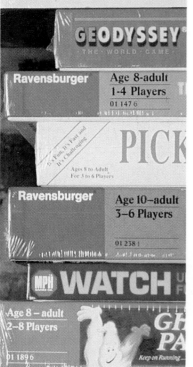

Board Games

Your group is part of Games Unlimited, Inc. Your assignment is to design a complex board game. Your game can be for two to six players and must include at least one random-generating device.

Select a theme for the game and create the graphic design of the game board on poster board. Develop instructions for the users of the game, complete with rules and objectives.

Due to a truth-in-advertising regulation, all game designers must explain the probability and odds of winning the game. They must also justify the fairness of the game to an inspecting agency. To satisfy this requirement, determine the probability and odds of winning your game and write a justification of the fairness of your game.

Plan and give an oral group presentation. Show your design to the class and give an explanation of the instructions. Demonstrate how to play the game. Give a detailed explanation of the probability and odds of winning the game and a justification of the fairness of the game.

WHAT'S FAIR IN REAL LIFE?

Chance is a part of life. Whether you are playing a game, staying healthy, entering a contest, buying insurance, or trying to be safe, there is chance involved. In mathematics, we use probability to evaluate our chances. The probability of an event occurring enables individuals, companies, and government to make certain decisions. For example, an insurance company makes decisions about the cost of premiums based on the probability of certain accidents occurring. An individual may make a decision about using an exploratory medical drug based on the likelihood of it benefiting them rather than harming them. Knowing your chances enables you to make informed decisions.

This investigation allows you, as a student, to investigate a situation that involves chance and payoff values. You may use many sources to find a topic and data. Many of these sources are available in the library. A few suggested sources are periodicals, encyclopedias, medical journals, consumer catalogs, almanacs, sport statistics, electronic bulletin boards, or databases.

The data you choose could be the odds of winning the lottery, insurance tables, sport or game odds, disease or medical information, or social data. Some ideas for topics are listed below, but do not feel restricted to this list.

- What are the odds of winning the lottery? What is the expected value of buying one ticket? Is it worth the cost of playing?
- What is the probability of dying from smoking? What are the costs involved?
- What is the probability that a house in Southern California will be destroyed by an earthquake? Compare the cost of the insurance to the cost of rebuilding the home.
- What is the probability that a major-league baseball team will be a division winner if most of their games are played away?

- What is the probability of a player hitting a grand slam in the ninth inning of a World Series game?
- What is the probability of getting a false-positive on a drug test compared to the probability of finding someone who actually is a drug user?

Select a topic and write a statement describing the need to analyze the situation using the data.

Determine the data that will help you analyze the problem. Interview someone outside of school and ask this person what he or she might consider in analyzing the problem situation.

Analyze the data using the tools in this unit: probability, odds, expected value, and so on. Determine your findings and conclusions.

Write a detailed report, including the following information.
- a description of the topic to be analyzed
- a background statement regarding the topic
- a statement of the need or the problem to solve
- a rationale for choosing the topic
- the raw data used to analyze the situation and the source of the data
- an explanation of the analysis of the data
- a description of the probability tools used in analyzing the data
- an interview with someone outside of school on the analysis of the situation
- all conclusions and findings
- graphs or charts depicting the data and supporting your conclusions
- a summary of the process you used in completing this task

Selection and Reflection

In this unit, the mathematical terms *probability, fairness, odds, expected value,* and *payoff value* were often used.

What do these terms mean?

What do these words mean in terms of the work you did in this unit?

Describe what you know about each of these terms, using examples from the unit to help you describe and define them.

WHAT THE ODDS ARE
A-to-Z Odds on Everything You Hoped or Feared Could Happen
LES KRANTZ

Marriage
Sex & Love
Longevity Rates
Lotteries
Casualties & Disasters
Rare Finds
Gambling
Health & Medicine
Thinking & Dreaming
Terrorism

Fair Play... Or Not?

The Problem

Scott and his sister, Julie, are tired of playing the games they have at home, so they decide to make up a new game. They place four marbles in a bag. Two are red and two are blue. They take turns drawing two marbles from the bag. If the marbles are the same color, Scott gets a point. If the marbles are different colors, Julie gets a point.

After each draw the marbles are put back in the bag. Is this game fair or unfair? Explain.

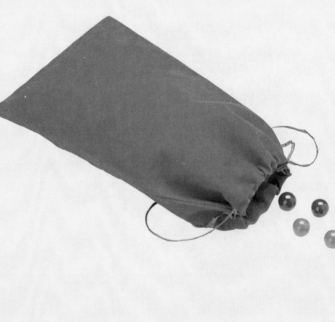

The Problem

Alfonso's dad takes Alfonso out to get a double dip of frozen yogurt for his birthday. The frozen yogurt shop offers a choice of six flavors: vanilla, chocolate, rocky road, strawberry, butter pecan, and mint chocolate chip. If Alfonso asks for two different flavors, what is the probability that he gets a scoop of chocolate and a scoop of mint chocolate chip? What is the probability that he gets this cone *and* the scoop of chocolate is on the bottom?

Color Me Pink

The Problem

Design a 4 × 4 checkerboard according to the clues listed below.

- The corner squares are all blue.
- The probability of dropping a pin and having its point land on a blue square is $\frac{3}{8}$.
- A blue square never touches another blue square on its side.
- A pink square never touches another pink square on its side.
- The probability of dropping a pin and having its point land on a pink square is $\frac{3}{8}$.
- All other squares are yellow.

Extension What is the probability of dropping a pin and having its point land on a yellow square?

The Problem

You and your friend have invented a new game called Crazy Cubes. To play the game, you roll two number cubes: one that has four sides numbered 1, 2, 3, and 4 and one that has six sides numbered 0, 1, 2, 3, 4, and 5. The object of the game is to roll both number cubes as many times as you want to get as close to, but not go over, a total score of 21. The person with the number of points closest to 21 is the winner. If you go over 21, you are disqualified and the other person automatically wins that round.

It is your turn. You have rolled the number cubes three times and your points add up to 18. Should you roll again to get closer to 21 or should you stop rolling and stay at 18 points? Explain your reasoning.

Are You A Leftie?

The Problem

The odds of having a left-handed child are 1 to 16 if neither parent is left-handed. If both parents are left-handed, the odds of having a left-handed child are *32 times as great*. What are the odds of two left-handed parents having a left-handed child? What is the probability of this occurring?

The Problem

The Hopi Indians invented a game of chance called Totolospi. This game was played with three cane dice, a counting board inscribed on stone, and a counter for each player. Each cane die can land round side up (R) or flat side up (F). In Totolospi for two players, each player places a counter on the nearest circle. The moves of the game are determined by tossing the three cane dice.

- Advance 2 lines with three round sides up (RRR).
- Advance 1 line with three flat sides up (FFF).
- Lose a turn with any other combination.

The player reaching the opposite side first wins.

If you are playing Totolospi with a friend, what is the probability that you will be able to advance your counter on the first toss?

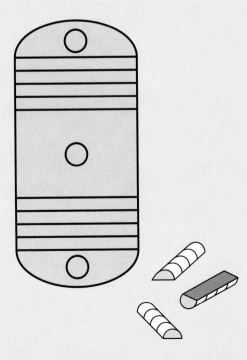

A Winning Combination

The Problem

The travel club at Girard Middle School has eight members. They raised enough money to pay for each member to go to Washington D.C., plus they had enough money left over to send three members to the state capitol for a weekend. They decide to have a drawing to determine who could go to the state capitol. Three names were chosen out of a hat. What is the probability that both you and your best friend in the club get to go on the trip?

TABLE OF CONTENTS

Game	Choose	From Digits	Number Correct	Payoff (on a $1 wager)
Pick 3 (straight)	3	0–9	3 in order	$500
Pick 3 (boxed)	3	0–9	3 in any order	3 different digits pays $83 3 digits with 2 the same pays $167
Pick 4 (straight)	4	0–9	4 in order	$5,000
Pick 4 (boxed)	4	0–9	4 in any order	4 different digits pays $200 4 digits with 2 the same pays $400 4 digits with 2 pairs the same pays $800 4 digits with 3 the same pays $1200
Buckeye 5	5	1–37	5	$100,000
Buckeye 5	5	1–37	4	$250
Buckeye 5	5	1–37	3	$10
Buckeye 5	5	1–37	2	$1
Super Lotto	6	1–47	6	varies, lowest jackpot is $4 million
Super Lotto	6	1–47	5	2.75% of sales
Super Lotto	6	1–47	4	8.59% of sales

Source: Ohio Lottery Commission

Note: If more than one person chooses 4, 5, or 6 numbers of the Super Lotto, the prize is divided equally among them. State law prohibits one winner from collecting more than $26 million on a Super Lotto prize.

The maximum payout for a Buckeye Five jackpot is $1 million. That means that up to ten people can win $100,000 for each drawing. If eleven winning tickets are sold for a drawing, each person would win $1,000,000 ÷ 11 or $90,909.

Cancer Death Rates by Site, U.S., 1930-1989

Females

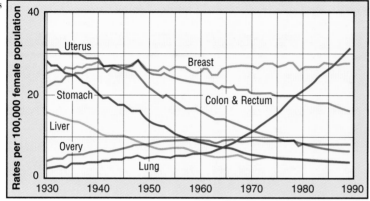

Males

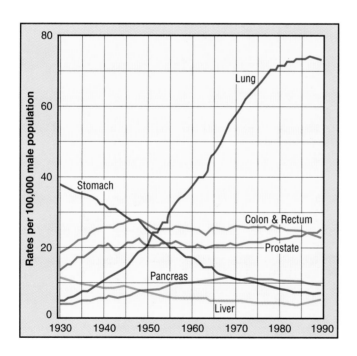

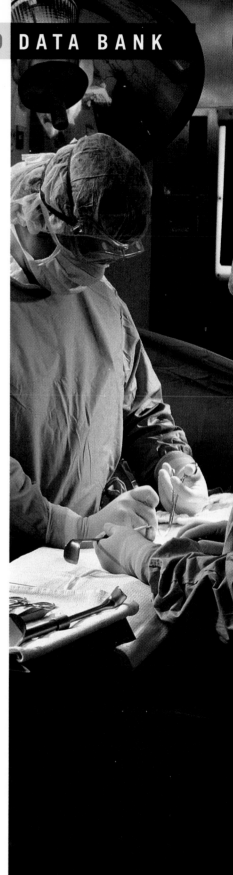

Source: American Cancer Society: rates adjusted to 1970 population

"Team of Scientists Contends Risk of California Quake is Overstated"

Government forecasts of disastrous earthquakes in California seriously exaggerate the risk, a team of scientists said today after using a computer to simulate 10,000 years of activity on the San Andreas Fault.

The new study suggests that the risk of a quake of 7.5 magnitude on the Richter scale or larger along the Southern California part of the fault is 19 percent within 30 years, said Dr. Steven Ward, a geophysicist at the University of California, Santa Cruz.

A forecast by the United States Geological Survey in 1988 said the odds were at least 60 percent in 30 years. The forecast was made and endorsed by panels representing a consensus of scientists. [Dr. Ward's] simulation suggested that big quakes happen almost randomly, rendering the government forecasts unreliable.

In little more than three years, three major quakes have hit California. The magnitude 7.1 Loma Prieta quake in 1989 killed 63 people in the San Francisco Bay region. The 7.1 Cape Medocino quake and its 6.7 and 6.6 aftershocks last April injured 356 people on the state's north coast. And on June 28, the 7.5 Landers quake and its 6.6 Big Bear aftershock killed a child and injured 402 Southern Californians. *(New York Times, December 9, 1992)*

Source: *Chance Magazine,* Winter 1993, p. 6

Home and Away Records for Major League Baseball Division Winners, 1969–1989		
	Number of Games	**Win Percentage**
Home	6,670	63.3
Away	6,680	55.3
All Games	13,350	59.3

Source: *Chance Magazine,* Spring 1993, p. 32

GLOSSARY INDEX

A

Accuracy, 16, 27
Actual outcomes, 23
Adds, 8
Algebra
    variables, 2
Analyze, 32
Average, 6

B

Basic program, 28
Boot, 28

C

Calculated, 6
Calculation, 2
Calculator, 6
Center, 17
Chance, 4, 5, 6, 15, 31, 39
Chances, 28
Charts, 32
Circle, 17
Column, 19
Combination, 39, 40
Compass, 16, 17, 26
Computer, 28, 29, 44
Computer program
    Chances, 28
Conclusion, 27, 28, 32
Cost, 31
Counting board, 39

D

Data, 29, 31, 32
    bank, 41-45
    bases, 31
Day, 5
Degrees, 17
Design, 30

Diagrams, 29
Distance, 2
Dividing, 5

E

Elevation, 2
Evaluate, 31
Even number, 10, 22
Event, 28 each round of a
    game played in a short
    amount of time
Events, 15, 27
Expected value, 7, 31, 32, 33
    helps to determine what is
    most likely to happen
Experimental odds, 21, 22

F

Fairness, 1, 8, 27, 28, 29, 30,
    33, 34
Forecast, 44
Fraction, 15, 17

G

Geometry
    center, 17
    circle, 17
    compass, 16, 17, 26
    distance, 2
    length, 2
    line, 9, 10, 11, 12, 13, 20,
        21, 22
    point, 17, 36
    protractor, 16, 17, 26
    radius, 17
    square, 17, 36
    vertical line, 17
Graphs, 29, 32

I

Inches, 17
Input, 28
Insurance tables, 31

L

Length, 2
Line, 9, 10, 11, 12, 13, 20, 21,
    22
Load, 28

M

Mathematics toolkit, 4-7
Measurement
    cost, 31
    day, 5
    degrees, 17
    distance, 2
    elevation, 2
    inches, 17
    length, 2
    months, 2
    size, 2
    speed, 2
    time, 28
    weight, 2
    years, 2, 44
Model, 16
Months, 2
Multiply, 17

N

Number, 5, 6, 9, 16, 17, 20, 21,
    25, 28
    cubes, 8, 10, 14, 20, 26
    even, 10, 22
    odd, 10

O

Odd number, 10
Odds, 1-45
    experimental, 21, 22
    theoretical, 21, 22
Outcome, 1

GLOSSARY INDEX

P

Pay-off value, 27, 28, 33
Percent, 6, 28, 44
Point, 17, 36
Predicted, 27
Probability, 1, 4, 5, 6, 14, 15,
    16, 18, 19, 20, 23, 24, 28, 30,
    31, 32, 33, 35, 36, 37, 38,
    40
    ratios, 1
    values, 1
Probable cause, 14-15
Problem solving, 1, 4, 7, 32
Protractor, 16, 17, 26

R

Radius, 17
Random-generating device,
    18, 27, 30
Random-generating spinners,
    1, 16
Randomly select, 14
Ratio, 19
Research, 3, 24

S

Scale, 16, 17
Sector of a circle, 17 part of a
    circle shaped like a piece of
    pie
Size, 2
Speed, 2
Square, 17, 36
Strategy, 18
Sum, 8, 10, 14, 26
Survey, 14

T

Table, 8
    insurance, 31
Tally mark, 19
Theoretical odds, 21, 22
Time, 28
Total, 5, 28

V

Variables, 2
Vertical line, 17

W

Weight, 2

Y

Years, 2, 44

PHOTO CREDITS

COVER: Todd Yarrington,

iii, 1(l), Tom Treick, (r), **2**(l), Richard Hamilton Smith/AllStock, (t), Tom Treick; **3**(t), BLT Productions/Brent Turner, (r), Richard Hamilton Smith/AllStock, (screened), Aaron Haupt Photography, (cl), Bill Ross/AllStock, (cr), Tom Treick, (bl), Culver Pictures, Inc, (br), Art Wolfe/AllStock; **4**(b), Richard Pasley/Stock Boston, (all others), BLT Productions/Brent Turner; **6, 7,** BLT Productions/Brent Turner, **8,** Bill Ross/Westlight; **9**(t), Matt Meadows, (b), Aaron Haupt Photography; **10,** Ross Hickson, **11**(l), BLT Productions/Brent Turner, (r), K S Studios/Bob Mullenix; **12, 13,** BLT Productions/Brent Turner; **14**(l), Bob Daemmrich/Stock Boston, (r), Aaron Haupt Photography; **15**(l), Brownie Harris/The Stock Market, (r), David Barnes/AllStock; **16**(l), Mark E. Gibson, (r), Aaron Haupt Photography; **18,** Matt Meadows; **19,** Rafael Macia/Photo Researchers; **21,** K S Studios/Bob Mullenix; **22,** Aaron Haupt Photography; **23,** Todd Yarrington; **24,** Rick Weber; **25,** Life Images; **26,** Doug Martin; **27, 28,** Life Images; **29,** BLT Productions/Brent Turner; **30,** Life Images; **31,** Don Smith/Sports Photo Masters; **32,** Robert W. Ginn/PhotoEdit; **33**(tl), Rick Weber, (tc), Gay Bumgarner/AllStock, (bl), Michael Furman/The Stock Market, (bc), David C. Bitters/Photo Resources, (r), Bachmann/Photo Researchers; **34**(l), Life Images, (r), K S Studios/Bob Mullenix; **35,** Elaine Comer-Shay; **36**(l), David Woods/The Stock Market, (r), Frank Oberle/Photo Resources; **38**(t), Michael Grecco/Stock Boston, (b), Life Images; **39,** David Young-Wolff/PhotoEdit; **40**(l), Lois Ellen Frank/Westlight, (r), Life Images; **41,** Roy Morsch/The Stock Market; **43,** Matthew Borkoski/Stock Boston; **44**(l), Sam Sargent/Photo Resources, (r), Vince Streano/The Stock Market; **45**(tl)(tc)(b), Aaron Haupt Photography, (r), Tom Ebenhoh/Photo Resources.